CONTENTS

Spectacular road, p. 12

WHAT'S HOT: SOUTH AFRICA

Where should you start your visit to South Africa? At one of the fantastic markets for a shopping trip? On a beautiful beach, warming yourself in the sun and snorkelling among the tropical fish? Or listening to *kwaito* music at a festival? It's hard to know where to begin – but these highlights should help you to decide.

Table Mountain cable car, p.13

1. RIDE THE CABLE CAR TO TABLE MOUNTAIN p.13

Cape Town is the first stopping place for many visitors, and you can't get a better view of the city than the one from Table Mountain.

2. CHUCK A *BOERIE* ON THE BRAAI p.16

The braai, or barbecue, is a favourite meal for most South Africans. Take along a boerie (sausage) or two, or maybe some prawns, and prepare to make some new friends. Just don't touch the braaier's tongs! Trying to muscle in on the person in charge of the barbecue is considered very bad form.

3. GIVE THE 'SMILEY' A MISS p.19

South Africa's snack food is fantastic, combining African, European and Asian ingredients and techniques. One local 'treat' you might want to miss out on, though is the 'Smiley' – a barbecued sheep's head. Apparently the eyes and the brain are the best bits...

4. DRIFT AWAY ON A RIVER OF SONG p.24

There are lots of great music festivals in South Africa, but Up The Creek is a festival with a difference. Bring along an inflatable rubber ring, and you can float along the river listening to the acts.

THE
REAL
SOUTH
AFRICA

Your need-to-know guide for all things South African

Moses Jones

700041451779

LONDON • SYDNEY

First published in 2014
by Franklin Watts

Franklin Watts
338 Euston Road
London NW1 3BH

Franklin Watts Australia
Level 17/207 Kent Street
Sydney, NSW 2000

Series editor: Sarah Peutrill
Series designer: Sophie Wilkins
Picture researcher: Diana Morris

Dewey number: 968'.068
HB ISBN: 978 1 4451 1975 5
Library ebook ISBN: 978 1 4451 2804 7

Printed in Malaysia

Franklin Watts is a division of Hachette
Children's Books, an Hachette UK company.
www.hachette.co.uk

Picture credits:
Africa Images/istockphoto: 5tl, 38tl, 38c.
Paul Alberts/Africa Media Online: 14t. Theo
Allfors/Corbis: 31. almond/Shutterstock:
front cover c. Lars Baron/Getty Images: 22c.
Henning de Beer/Shutterstock: 6tl, 8t, 48.
Gerry Bougham/Shutterstock: 38tc, 40t,
42tc. Neil Bradfield/Shutterstock: 5bl, 12tc,
12b. coolendelkid/istockphoto: front cover
br. Dominique de la Croix/Shutterstock: 1,
30tr, 30b. Daly & Newton//Getty Images:
16tl, 17b. DStv: 26. EPA/Alamy: 41t. Inna
Felker/Shutterstock: 35t, 47. fsstockfoto/
Shutterstock: 38tr, 38b. Gallo Images/Getty
Images: 25b. Roger de la Harpe/Africa Media
Online: 20b, 32, 33br. Per Andre Hoffman/
Getty Images: 42tl. Images of Africa/
Alamy: 41b. JG Photo/Shutterstock: 7t, 34t.
Alexander Joe/AFP/Getty Images: 23. Michael
Jung/Shutterstock: 5tc, 6tr, 11t, 12tr, 12c.
kaarsten/Shutterstock: 29. Sue Kramer/
Africa Media Online: 12tl, 15. David Larsen/
Africa Media Online: 14b. Martin Maritz/
Shutterstock: 35b. Henrique NDR Martins/
istockphoto: 22tr, 28t, 42tr. Meunierd/
Shutterstock: 10b. Belia Oh Photography:
22tl, 24t. ollyy/Shutterstock: front cover bc.
Photosky/Shutterstock: 2, 6c, 30tl, 34b.
Valerry Pistryy/Dreamstime: front cover t. G
du Preez: 5tr, 33bl. Radius Images/Alamy:
18c. Kelvin Saunders/Getty Images for HSBC:
10tr. Kirstin Scholtz/ASP/Getty Images:
40b. Elzbieta Sekowska/Shutterstock: 16tr,
18b. Emir Simsek/Shutterstock: 24b. Martin
Strimska/Alamy: 37. Guy Stubbs/Africa Media
Online: 28b. Elena Talberg/Shutterstock: 6tc,
9t. Kasia Wandycz/Paris Match/Getty Images:
16tc, 20t. Roger Ward/Africa Media Online:
39. Paul Weinberg/South Photos/Africa Media
Online: 19b. Graeme Williams/South Photos/
Africa Media Online: 19t. Wingnut films: 27.
Kymri Witt/Alamy: 19c. Andrew Woodburn/
Africa Media Online: 36. Anke van Wykke/
Dreamstime: front cover bl. Anke van Wyk/
Shutterstock: 16c.

Every attempt has been made to clear
copyright. Should there be any inadvertent
omission please apply to the publisher for
rectification.

5. FOLLOW IN THE FOOTSTEPS OF THE *STRANDLOPERS* p.32

The first *strandlopers* were African tribes-people, who walked the shores of the Wild Coast looking for food. You can follow in their footsteps with this five-day hike along one of South Africa's most beautiful shores.

6. HANG OUT WITH THE LOCALS (THEY'RE A BUNCH OF BABOONS) p.34

Baboons have been hanging out around Cape Town longer than people, so it's no wonder they treat the place like home. They empty bins, steal food and even invade someone's house once in a while.

7. JOIN THE CROWD AT SOCCER CITY p.38

Whether you're here to see the national team (nickname *Bafana Bafana*, or 'the boys, the boys') or the Kaizer Chiefs (nickname *Amakhosi*, or 'the lords'), the stadium will be jumping with the cheers of over 90,000 spectators.

Cape Town locals, p.34

IT'S (NEARLY) OFFICIAL!
TOP PLACES TO VISIT IN SOUTH AFRICA

1. Cape Town – actually voted the WORLD'S best destination in 2011, for its combination of city life, beaches and beautiful natural environment.

2. Knysna – between the mountains and the Indian Ocean, Knysna has twice been voted South Africa's favourite town. People are drawn here by the beautiful lagoon and the lovely forest.

3. Kruger National Park – the oldest wildlife park in Africa is just 5 hours north of Johannesburg, and is a great place to see African animals in their native habitat.

4. Durban – a favourite holiday spot for South Africans, because of the wonderful beaches and warm water. The city has a large Indian population, and a visit to the Indian Street Market makes a great afternoon out.

5. Drakensberg – great for outdoor sports such as hiking and rock climbing; also good for amateur archaeologists, here to see the ancient Bushman rock art.

6. Hermanus – this seaside town is close to South Africa's most southerly point, and a brilliant place for whale watching. You can also try surfing, kayaking or – if you're feeling bold – cage diving with great white sharks.

SOUTH AFRICA FACTS AND STATS

Giant's Castle, Drakensberg Mountains

South Africa has something for just about everyone. Thrill seekers can swim with great white sharks or plunge down steep slopes on a mountain bike. Nature lovers may spot lions, elephants, buffaloes and more. There's a whole holiday's worth of fun for foodies, shopaholics and music fans, too.

LANDSCAPE

South Africa's landscape has three key features: the huge plateau that makes up most of the interior, the line of hills at its fringe and the coastal regions. South Africa has over 2,500 km of coastline, and is a beach-lover's paradise.

In most places, just a short distance inland from the sea you come to a line of mountainous hills, called the Great Escarpment. Here the land rises up into peaks, before dropping down again towards the interior. The highest point of the Great Escarpment is the Drakensberg, whose name means 'Dragon Mountains' in Afrikaans.

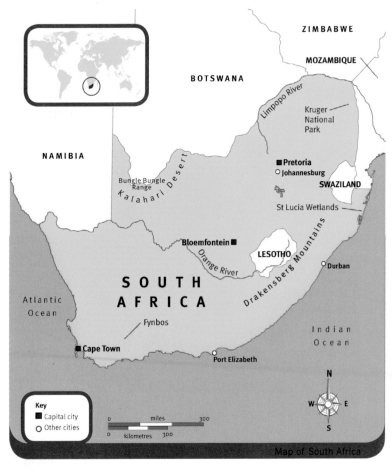

Map of South Africa

CLIMATE

South Africa's climate is different on the west and east coasts. A cold ocean current, the Benguela Current, brushes the west coast and keeps temperatures lower. On the east coast, the warm Agulhas Current has the opposite effect.

The good news for travellers is that each year, South Africa gets only a little more than half the world average amount of rain: 460mm v. 860mm.

Overall the temperature is rarely uncomfortably hot or cold, but the best times to visit are probably spring (August to mid October) or autumn (mid February to April). In spring the flowers and wildlife are at their most spectacular. In autumn there is little rain, the days are hot and sunny, and at night it is warm.

"South Africa is the most beautiful country I have been to."

— Honor Blackman, well-travelled English actress and Bond girl

Spring flowers on the west coast

FACT FILE ONE

CAPITAL CITY: Pretoria (Tshwane) is the administrative capital, from which the country is run. Cape Town is the legislative capital and Bloemfontein is the judicial capital

AREA: 1,214,470 km² (land territory), plus 4,620 km² (ocean territory)

HIGHEST MOUNTAIN: Njesuthu (3,408 m)

LOWEST POINT: Atlantic Ocean (0 m)

LONGEST RIVER: Orange River (2,200 km)

BORDERS: Botswana, Lesotho (an independent country inside the borders of South Africa), Mozambique, Namibia, Swaziland, Zimbabwe

NATURAL HAZARDS: drought

ONE COUNTRY, MANY PEOPLES

The first people in the region came from several different African tribal groups, such as the Xhosa. Next, Dutch settlers arrived – one of South Africa's main languages, Afrikaans, is descended from Dutch. Soon after, English, Indian and Chinese came. All these peoples and more make up the population of modern South Africa.

Young rugby fans

APARTHEID

In the recent past, a white-controlled government separated South Africans according to their race, in a system called 'apartheid' (see pages 14–15 to find out more). Whites got the best places to live, jobs and other privileges. Apartheid ended in 1994 and today, all South Africa's peoples have equal rights.

Poor housing in a Cape Town 'township'

DIFFICULTIES AND DANGERS

South Africa is a beautiful country, where the people have a great appetite for fun and enjoying life. Nonetheless, there are problems that can affect travellers. The biggest is crime. The money and possessions travellers carry regularly lead to violent robberies. Tourist areas during daylight are generally safe, but exploring alone at night is a bad idea. It is best never to show people if you have valuable items, such as cameras, jewellery, or large amounts of money.

There are also health risks in South Africa. The sun can be strong, and may cause sunburn or even sunstroke. A few areas, especially around the Kruger National Park, have the dangerous disease malaria. And South Africa has one of the highest HIV infection rates in the world.

Aerial view of Durban

> "I owe my being to the hills and the valleys, the mountains and the glades, the rivers, the deserts, the trees, the flowers, the seas and the ever-changing seasons that define the face of our native land."
>
> — Former President of South Africa Thabo Mbeki, 1996

FACT FILE TWO

POPULATION: 48.6 million

MAJOR CITIES: Johannesburg (3.6 million), Cape Town (3.4 million), Ekurhuleni (East Rand) (3.1 million), Durban (2.8 million), Pretoria (1.4 million)

AGE STRUCTURE: 28.3% under 15 years old; 65.6% 15–64 years old; 6.1% over 64 years old

YOUTH UNEMPLOYMENT (15–24 year-olds): 49.8%

OBESITY: 31.3%

LANGUAGES: South Africa has 11 official languages, including isiZulu, isiXhosa, Afrikaans, Sepedi and English. Most people know more than one language, and many South Africans can speak English.

RELIGIONS: Christianity (79.7%), Islam (1.5%)

CAPE TOWN

Cape Town is the first place many visitors head for when they arrive in South Africa. The city is not far from the southern tip of Africa, where the Atlantic and Indian oceans meet. Cape Town is spread out beside Table Bay, and looming above it is the famous Table Mountain.

Cape Town is at the foot of Table Mountain

Chapman's Peak Drive, one of South Africa's most spectacular roads

CHAPMAN'S PEAK DRIVE

Pretty much anyone in Cape Town will tell you Chapman's Peak Drive is the city's prettiest road. It hugs a cliff face above the Atlantic Ocean: rock falls and bad weather often stop the traffic. You can drive, cycle or walk along it.

At the end of the drive is a bronze statue of a leopard, one of the wild animals that once roamed the area. Fortunately for visitors (but unfortunately for the leopards), many of these wild creatures no longer exist on the Cape.

TOP DISTRICTS TO VISIT

Cape Town has many different districts, but the map on the right shows a few places where you could start to explore the city.

> "This is a pretty and singular town; it lies at the foot of an enormous wall [Table Mountain], which reaches into the clouds, and makes a most imposing barrier."
>
> — Charles Darwin, naturalist and scientist, 1836

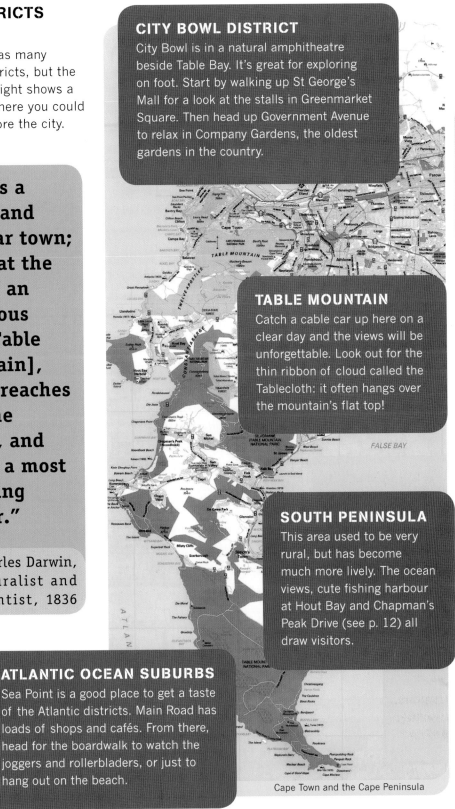

CITY BOWL DISTRICT

City Bowl is in a natural amphitheatre beside Table Bay. It's great for exploring on foot. Start by walking up St George's Mall for a look at the stalls in Greenmarket Square. Then head up Government Avenue to relax in Company Gardens, the oldest gardens in the country.

TABLE MOUNTAIN

Catch a cable car up here on a clear day and the views will be unforgettable. Look out for the thin ribbon of cloud called the Tablecloth: it often hangs over the mountain's flat top!

SOUTH PENINSULA

This area used to be very rural, but has become much more lively. The ocean views, cute fishing harbour at Hout Bay and Chapman's Peak Drive (see p. 12) all draw visitors.

ATLANTIC OCEAN SUBURBS

Sea Point is a good place to get a taste of the Atlantic districts. Main Road has loads of shops and cafés. From there, head for the boardwalk to watch the joggers and rollerbladers, or just to hang out on the beach.

Cape Town and the Cape Peninsula

VISITING SOUTH AFRICA'S PAST

South Africa is a modern country, one of the wealthiest in Africa. Black, white and other people mix together freely, and have equal rights. Not so long ago, though, a policy called apartheid meant this wasn't the case.

A pre-removals family in District 6

The District 6 Museum, Cape Town

VISITING THE
DISTRICT 6 MUSEUM

The District 6 Museum in Cape Town is a good place to learn what apartheid was once like. District 6 was an area mainly lived in by 'coloured' South Africans (see p. 15). But in 1966, the government decided District 6 should be a whites-only area. It began removing the non-white people who lived there.

By 1982, over 60,000 people had been forced to move. They were mostly sent to the Cape Flats Township, a bleak area 25 km away. Their homes were bulldozed.

Today, the museum is a moving reminder of how the removals affected people. You can read handwritten notes from the residents, visit rooms set out as if people still live there, see photographs and listen to recordings of people speaking about what happened.

APARTHEID

Apartheid began in 1948 and ended in 1994. During this time, white South Africans controlled the government, police and army. All South Africans were separated into racial groups: Black, White, Indian or Coloured.

Each group had to live in its own area. Basically, whites got the best areas, and non-whites got the rest. Black people were forced to move to their 'homelands' (which many of them had never seen before), or live in 'townships' – poor areas near to cities.

> "Visit Cape Town and history is never far from your grasp. It lingers in the air, a scent on the breeze."
>
> — Tahir Shah, travel writer, in *Travels With Myself*

RESIDENTS RETURN

When apartheid ended, the new government said that the area's old inhabitants should be able to return. In 2004, former president Nelson Mandela gave the keys of new homes to the first two people to come back and live in District 6.

OTHER PLACES TO VISIT

Two more places where you can see how apartheid affected the people of South Africa:

1. Robben Island, Cape Town

This island in Table Bay is where many anti-apartheid campaigners, including Nelson Mandela (right) were imprisoned. You can catch a tour-boat from the V&A Waterfront in Cape Town.

2. Apartheid Museum, Johannesburg

Opened in 2001, the museum explains the twentieth-century history of South Africa, particularly the apartheid years.

BRAAI

Braai is South African for barbecue. A braai isn't just a meal – it's also a big social event. During the summer in particular, the evening air is filled with the smell and sounds of people having a braai, enjoying cooking and eating their meal outside. Braai is so popular, though, that it happens throughout the year.

A traditional braai

GOING TO A BRAAI

What can you expect if you're invited to a braai? Usually everyone joins in to provide part of the feast, so guests will bring something to put on the braai, a side dish, or both. The barbecued food will be mostly meat, but if you're near the sea there might be fresh fish or giant prawns sizzling on the grill. Salads, bread and perhaps pap, a kind of maize porridge, will be served alongside.

WATCH OUT FOR THE MONKEYGLAND SAUCE!

If you attend a braai or eat meat in a restaurant, someone is almost sure to ask you if you'd like some 'monkeygland sauce' on your meat. Yeuw!

Actually, monkeygland sauce is not as bad as it sounds. It's a spicy sauce based on tomato, onion and fruit. No monkeys are harmed in its making. The sauce you DO need to watch out for is *chakalaka* – it's so hot it makes tears spring from your eyes.

BRAAI DAY

Braai Day is a celebration of South Africa's favourite type of meal, the barbecue. Across the country (and around the world), South Africans get together to cook food on a fire. Braai Day is held on National Heritage Day, 24 September.

BRAAI COOKING ETIQUETTE

At a braai (just like at barbecues all round the world), it is almost always men who cook the meat. In charge of everything there will probably be one man, called the braaier.

The key rule at a braai is: **DO NOT TOUCH THE BRAAIER'S MEAT, COALS, TONGS OR ANYTHING ELSE** unless expressly asked to. He will get really annoyed.

"Across race, language, region and religion, we all share a common heritage... when we have something to celebrate, we light fires and prepare great feasts."

— from the National Braai Day mission statement

FOOD AND SHOPPING

Friends enjoy an evening braai

SNACK FOOD FAVOURITES

S nack food is one of the great things about visiting another country. Of course, everywhere in the world you can get burgers or pizza if you're feeling homesick. But the really fun thing is checking out the snacks and treats you CAN'T get at home.

TOP PICKS
One of the best things about South Africa's food is the way it use spices and flavours from different parts of the world. Here are a few treats from the streets:

1. *Vetkoek*
You see this being sold on lots of city street corners, often at boerie roll stalls. Vetkoek is a deep-fried doughy snack, a bit like a doughnut. They're usually filled with minced beef, syrup, honey or jam.

2. *Boerie* roll
The most popular snack in South Africa? Possibly. *Boerie* is short for boerewors, or sausage. These are basically hotdogs, but made with a juicy, spiced-meat sausage and served with a tomato-and-onion sauce called 'train smash'.

A meaty vetkoek snack

WHAT'S IN A NAME?

Boerewors is South Africa's favourite kind of sausage. It gets its name from two words. Boer is the name for the original Dutch farmers who settled in South Africa, and *wors* is sausage. The boers took dried boerewors with them on their long treks north into Africa.

Boerewors sausage on the grill

THREE SOUTH AFRICAN SPECIALITIES YOU MAY NOT WANT TO TRY...

The Smiley

1. The Smiley

This is a barbecued sheep's head, usually served with a litre of fizzy drink and half a loaf of bread. Fans say that the eyeballs and brains are the best bits. The name comes from the sheep's grin once its lips have been burned off in the braai.

2. Walkie-talkies

Made of chicken's feet ('walkie') and head ('talkie'). They're boiled to remove the tough outer layer of skin, rubbed with spices, salt and pepper, then grilled.

Mopane worms

3. Mopane worms

These are actually large caterpillars, not worms. They have their insides squeezed out before being laid in the sun to dry. Then they're eaten raw, or mixed with tomato and chilli sauce.

3. The Gatsby

This is a Cape Town speciality that is now popular across the country. It's a long bread roll filled with meat (usually masala steak, which has been soaked in spices before being cooked, or processed sausage), chips, cheese and salad.

4. Bunny chow

This originally came from Durban, a city with a large Indian community. Bunny chow is a hollowed-out half loaf of white bread, filled with hot sauce, pickles and/or curry.

Bunny chow

NO bunnies are harmed in the making of this dish – unless the curry is rabbit curry.

FLEA MARKETS

Wandering around a South African flea market is great fun if you like picking your way through a huge variety of products. You'll find anything from used cookers to traditional handicrafts and fake Cartier watches.

Browsing at Rosebank Market, Johannesburg

TOP TIPS FOR MARKET VISITS

1. Feel free to haggle

Unless you're buying food, the first price the seller gives you is usually negotiable. A smiling, friendly approach often works best if you're trying to get the cost down.

2. Watch your bags

Most people are honest, but thieves do haunt some markets. Make sure your bag and money are secure.

Bright colours at the Victoria Street Market, Durban

TAKE A JOHANNESBURG FLEA-MARKET TOUR

Johannesburg used to be home to the Bruma Lake Market, which claimed to be the biggest flea market in the southern hemisphere. It has now gone, but fortunately there are plenty more flea markets in Johannesburg. Our three-market tour starts in the north of the city.

African Craft Market, Rosebank

Attractions: craft stalls, food, live music

Traders from all over Africa come here to sell their goods, and it's especially good for West African products. The food here – smoked meat, cheese and local specialities – is great too.

Market Theatre Flea Market

Attractions: fashion stalls, live music and dance displays

From Rosebank, head for the city centre. Here you'll find the Market Theatre Flea Market, which claims to be Johannesburg's original flea market. Young designers often bring their products here, so it's a good place to pick up some of the latest clothes, jewellery or fabrics.

Panorama Flea Market, Alberton

Attractions: varied stalls, food area, live music

In the south of Johannesburg, Panorama is open on Saturdays, Sundays and public holidays. There are over 350 stalls, selling everything from clothes and jewellery to dolls' houses.

TWO MORE GREAT MARKETS

1. Neighbourgoods Market, Cape Town

When: Saturday mornings
Where: The Old Biscuit Mill, Woodstock
Surely Cape Town's trendiest market, you can buy fresh food straight from the people who grew/caught/reared it and there are also food stalls run by top local chefs.

2. Victoria Street Market, Durban

The Victoria Street Market is a short walk from the heart of the local Indian community. It's a great place to smell Asian spices or try out Asian fabrics and clothes. The fish market downstairs is a foodie's dream.

POP MUSIC – FROM BUBBLEGUM TO KWAITO

Nianell (in the red dress) is one of South Africa's biggest music stars

South Africa has a big music scene. Fiddle with a radio for ten minutes and you'll hear just about every style of music you know, and probably a few new ones. The music scene is particularly strong in four cities: Cape Town, Johannesburg, Durban and Bloemfontein. Each is loyal to its local musicians and producers.

A LITTLE BIT OF HISTORY

The 1980s – this is when 'bubblegum' first appeared. It is light, dance-oriented pop music that combines American-style disco, jazz and African beats. It was the apartheid era, though, and the poppy sound didn't stop the songs from having titles such as *Vulindlela* ('make way').

The 1990s – around the world house music was everywhere, and South African musicians adapted it to their own taste.

They combined house and bubblegum, slowed down the beat and added drum loops and chanted or shouted lyrics. The result was kwaito. This is still the most popular form of music in the country today.

2000s and on – young South African musicians have started blending sounds again, this time mixing kwaito with traditional African tribal singing, drumbeats and other noises.

SOUTH AFRICAN SOUNDS PLAYLIST

You should be able to find these on music-streaming sites or YouTube.

1. Brenda Fassie and Papa Wemba: 'Ngiyaktuhanda' ('I love you') The queen of South African music, singing a duet with one of West Africa's biggest stars.

2. Boom Shaka: 'It's About Time' The band has now split, but they were one of the biggest early kwaito acts. It's also worth searching for songs by Lebo Mathosa, one of the lead singers, who launched a solo career in 2000.

3. Lucky Dube: 'Respect' Dube was the leading musician in South Africa's reggae/dancehall scene until his death in a suspected carjacking in 2007.

4. Mandosa: 'Bean Town Minute' The South African Jay-Z? Possibly – a big rap star in South Africa and beyond, anyway.

BRENDA FASSIE

Brenda Fassie was known as 'The Madonna of the Townships'. She was the original queen of bubblegum music. Almost as famous for her outrageous personal life as her music, she later became a big kwaito star – one of few women making kwaito. She died in 2004.

'The Madonna of the Townships', Brenda Fassie

"I am a shocker, I like to create controversy. It's my trademark."

"I'm going to become the Pope next year. Nothing is impossible."

— Both quotes are from Brenda Fassie (who never did become Pope).

FIVE MUSIC FESTIVALS

South Africa's warm climate is ideal for outdoor music, especially in spring or autumn. There's hardly any chance of a festival becoming a Glastonbury-style mudfest! Any of these five festivals would be a good place to start your musical journey through the country.

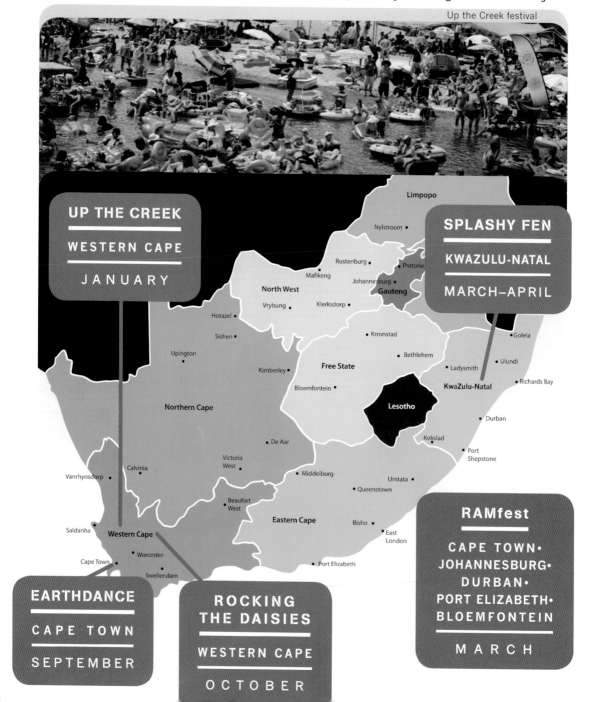

Up the Creek festival

UP THE CREEK
WESTERN CAPE
JANUARY

SPLASHY FEN
KWAZULU-NATAL
MARCH–APRIL

RAMfest
CAPE TOWN·
JOHANNESBURG·
DURBAN·
PORT ELIZABETH·
BLOEMFONTEIN
MARCH

EARTHDANCE
CAPE TOWN
SEPTEMBER

ROCKING THE DAISIES
WESTERN CAPE
OCTOBER

Limpopo
Nylstroom
Rustenburg
Mafikeng
Pretoria
North West
Johannesburg
Gauteng
Vrybung
Klerksdorp
Hotazel
Sishen
Krronstad
Golela
Upington
Bethlehem
Ulundi
Kimberley
Free State
Ladysmith
Bloemfontein
KwaZulu-Natal
Richards Bay
Northern Cape
Lesotho
Durban
De Aar
Kokslad
Victoria West
Port Shepstone
Calvinia
Middelburg
Vanrhynsdorp
Umtata
Queenstown
Beaufort West
Eastern Cape
Bisho
Saldanha
Western Cape
East London
Worcester
Cape Town
Port Elizabeth
Swellendam

SOUTH AFRICAN FESTIVAL PLANNER

Here are some of the best music festivals in South Africa.

JANUARY:

Up the Creek
(Western Cape)

This is a festival with a twist: if you bring some kind of inflatable device, you can float about in the creek while listening to the acts. Up The Creek is a relatively small festival, and features mainly folk, indie and rock bands.

MARCH–APRIL:

Splashy Fen
(KwaZulu-Natal)

This is said to be the oldest festival in South Africa, and it's one of the best for families. You get to see plenty of music, but there is also paintballing, ziplines, whitewater tube-riding on the river, and more. The music is a real mixture: ska, folk, acoustic, drum-and-bass and electro dance.

SEPTEMBER:

Earthdance
(Cape Town)

Earthdance is part of a huge global music event: in 2012 there were over 300 Earthdances, spread across more than 60 countries. Key features include:
• A lot of dancing
• A prayer for the planet
• The same song being played at the same time at all the Earthdance festivals going on around the world.

MARCH:

RAMfest
(Cape Town/Johannesburg/ Durban/Port Elizabeth/ Bloemfontein)

If you love metal, this is the festival for you. If you don't, it probably isn't – though non-metal acts do play. In 2013, the Durban version of RAMfest* was split into separate rock/metal and electronic dates. The festival is held at various locations around South Africa, so wherever you are there should be a version of it fairly nearby.

*RAM stands for Real Alternative Music.

OCTOBER:

Rocking The Daisies
(Western Cape)

The biggest star of this festival is the beautiful location, in the mountains of the Western Cape. On stage, local indie, folk and rock acts rub shoulders with big international bands. Rocking The Daisies is famous for its brilliant food stalls. The festival also features a comedy tent, a cinema tent and a beach bar (which is at least 10 km from a beach).

MUSIC AND LEISURE

TV, MOVIES AND SOCIAL MEDIA

Contestants in the popular TV show *Masterchef South Africa*

South Africans spend their leisure time in similar ways to other people around the world. Young people hang out with their friends, at cafés, on the beach, or shopping malls. Almost everyone watches TV and listens to the radio, and people also enjoy going to the cinema. As Internet access improves, social media are also becoming increasingly popular.

TV IN SOUTH AFRICA

Amazingly, South Africa only got its first TV channel in 1976*. Today, though, South Africans can choose from a wide range of digital or satellite TV channels. Reality TV shows are popular, including:

- *Idols*, which aims to find the country's best young singer
- *Masterchef South Africa* (above), which searches for the best cook
- *Top Billing*, which shows off the lifestyles of the rich and famous.

*The apartheid government thought TV would be a bad influence, and for a long time refused to allow it.

SOCIAL NETWORKING

The most popular social network in South Africa, especially with young people, has been Mxit (pronounced 'mix it'). However, Facebook and Twitter are rapidly catching up with Mxit, because many new phones are sold with these pre-installed.

TOP MOVIES SET IN SOUTH AFRICA

There are lots of great films set in South Africa, but this list is a good place to start – whether you want politics, sport or sci-fi:

Tsotsi (2006)

When Tsotsi steals a car, he gets a bit more than he bargained for. There's a baby inside, and he has to look after it. Set in the townships of Johannesburg, *Tsotsi* (which is local slang for 'thug') won an Oscar for Best Foreign Language Film.

Invictus (2009)

The story of South Africa's attempt to win the 1995 Rugby World Cup on home soil. President Nelson Mandela helped the team to become a symbol of South African unity after apartheid.

District 9 (2009)

Directed by Peter Jackson, this is a slightly bonkers sci-fi movie. It tells the story of a group of extraterrestrial refugees who take shelter in District 9, Johannesburg. The film was partly inspired by the mass evictions in District 6, Cape Town (see pages 14–15).

MUSIC AND LEISURE

A clip from the sci-fi movie *District 9*

QUIRKY FESTIVALS

As well as big holidays and festivals such as Christmas, there are lots of smaller local festivals in South Africa. Heading off to one of these for the day or the weekend is a popular leisure activity for South Africans. This is just a small selection of locals' tips for quirky festivals to attend.

Face painting at Ficksburg Cherry Festival

THE GUMBOOT DANCE

Gumboots are big rubber workboots. The gumboot dance (right) is a foot-stomping dance, developed by black workers during the apartheid era. Today it is taught in many schools, and you see it at festivals and tourist venues around South Africa.

HANTAM VLEISFEES

CALVINIA, NORTHERN CAPE

AUGUST

This is definitely not a festival for vegetarians: its name is Afrikaans for 'meat feast'. Amongst the other attractions – which include a music concert and a street party – there's a LOT of meat eating. Whether you want to try meat cooked on a braai, curried, stewed, served in pitta, made into *sosaties* (lamb kebabs), or cooked in a *potjie* (a traditional cast-iron pot), you'll find it here.

ELLISRAS BUSHVELD FESTIVAL

LIMPOPO

JULY

Bushveld is a typical South African landscape: hot, dry and dusty, with thorn trees and scrub. This festival is a great place to get into the lifestyle of bushveld farming communities. There are cattle and dog shows, horse jumping contests, a best 4x4 competition, traditional food and huge campfires at night.

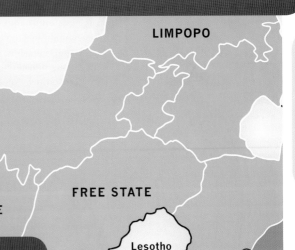

LIMPOPO

FREE STATE

NORTHERN CAPE

Lesotho

Durban

EASTERN CAPE

Cape Town

FICKSBURG CHERRY FESTIVAL

FREE STATE

NOVEMBER

Ficksburg is a small place with a big claim: the town says it's the 'Cherry Capital of the World'. There are cherry tastings, picnics and music, but the real star is the surrounding scenery. Ficksburg is close to the border with the mountain kingdom of Lesotho, and the landscape here is famous for its amazing sandstone formations.

PRICKLY PEAR FESTIVAL

UITENHAGE, EASTERN CAPE

FEB/MAR

Prickly pears have come a long way since 1937, when the authorities branded them 'alien undesirables' that had to be wiped out. Today they have their own festival, where you can buy prickly pear jams, prickly pear pickles and even prickly pear *witblits*, a drink that was once illegal.

CAMPING AND THE OUTDOOR LIFE

S outh Africa is a great place for spending time outdoors. It has great weather, beautiful scenery, an incredible variety of wildlife, and the freshest food and drink. That's probably why so many South Africans enjoy packing up on a Friday night and heading off for a weekend's camping.

Field of flowers in Namaqualand

TOP PLACES TO CAMP

Whether you want to camp beside a river, up a *kloof* (canyon), on a beach or in the bush, there are hundreds of great campsites in South Africa. These three will give you a taste of what's available:

Fiddler's Creek campsite, Namaqualand

This area is famous for the colours that spring up after autumn rains. You can head out on 4x4 trips to wilderness camping areas, or go whitewater rafting.

Coffee Shack Backpackers, Eastern Cape

On the beautiful Wild Coast (see pages 32–33), Coffee Shack is at the mouth of the Bomvu River. Learn to surf, take a three-day drumming course or hike through the beautiful surrounding area.

Matroosberg Private Nature Reserve, Western Cape

Best avoided in winter, perhaps (you're likely to get snow), there's great abseiling, rock climbing, mountain biking and hiking here. Top pick is probably *kloofing*, the South African version of canyoning. Kloofing involves sliding, swimming, abseiling and jumping your way down a steep, narrow ravine.

CAMP SAFE

Tents cannot be locked against intruders, so it's generally safest to camp in private 'caravan parks' (which also take tents) and municipal parks. There are lots of these in busy coastal tourist areas.

Unless you are in a large, organised group, wild camping is generally not a good idea. You risk being robbed – and if the criminals don't get you, the wildlife might.

CAMPING SURVIVAL CHECKLIST

This is a list of the must-take stuff for a good night's sleep:

- Tent, sleep mat, sleeping bag, pillow
- Plenty of food and water, plus a camping stove if anything will need to be heated
- Bug repellent, especially in mosquito/malaria areas, possibly a mosquito net, wash gear, and a torch.

LANDSCAPE AND NATURE

Campsite by the sea, Tsitsikamma National Park

HIKING THE WILD COAST

Hikers follow a coastal trail in the Eastern Cape region

Southern Africa's Wild Coast lives up to its name. Waves crash on to the beaches and against the headlands. Rivers race down to the sea. To the south are wide, shark-haunted river mouths. To the north some rivers fling themselves from cliffs as waterfalls.

WHAT'S A STRANDLOPER?

The first strandloper were the African tribespeople who wandered along this shore gathering food. Strandloper comes from two Afrikaans words: *strand*, which means beach, and *loper*, meaning walker. So a strandloper is a beach wanderer.

THE STRANDLOPER TRAIL

Walking is one of the best ways to see the Wild Coast. The Strandloper trail is a five-day walk along the Wild Coast. You have to wade across rivers, hike along sandy beaches, tramp up and over headlands, go through steamy milkwood forests and walk over rocky wave platforms.

The trail goes from Cape Morgan to Gonubie. At the overnight stops*, you can cook a meal before having a well-earned sleep.

*You have to pre-book a place at these.

First night

You sleep in an old pumping station, where saltwater used to be pumped up to a nearby mine. The old pump is still inside!

WRECK OF THE SANTO ESPIRITU

On day 3 of the Strandloper trail, you might notice little pieces of pottery in the sand near the mouth of the Quko River. They came from the Portuguese ship *Santo Espiritu*, which was wrecked nearby in 1608.

Third night

At Cape Henderson you turn off the trail a short way along, to reach a log cabin with bunks inside.

Fourth night

You sleep in a basic hut: four rooms, with 12 bunks. But day four is a long walk, and there's a longer one tomorrow, so you'll be too tired to worry!

Pumphouse accommodation

Second night

Your bed tonight is in an old hikers' hut at Double Mouth. Outside is a covered braai, so don't forget your boerewors (sausages).

Wading a river

AN ANIMAL-SPOTTER'S PARADISE

Cape Town locals hold up the traffic

Southe Africa is home to some amazing animals. It you've ever hoped to rub shoulders with a lion (not literally!), cheetah, elephant or gazelle, this is a great place to do it. You don't even have to visit a game reserve or zoo. Everywhere you look, there are all kinds of wildlife.

TWO CITY ANIMALS TO WATCH FOR

Near to Cape Town, you're quite likely to see baboons. They look cute, but baboons are powerful, occasionally bad-tempered animals that sometimes attack humans.

Near to beaches you ften see African penguins*. The peng   seem to like living near humans: a who   olony moved to a busy beach near Cape Tow. in the mid-1980s.

*Also known as jackass or black-footed penguins.

... AND SOME MORE TO REALLY WATCH OUT FOR

There are quite a few dangerous animals lurking around South Africa. As well as the 'Big Five' (see next page), keep an eye out for crocodiles, great white sharks, bull sharks and deadly snakes such as puff adders, boomslangs, and green and black mambas.

More Cape Town locals

THE 'BIG FIVE'

Many people come to Africa hoping to spot the 'Big Five' animals: lion, leopard, rhino, elephant and Cape buffalo. The Big Five originally got their name from hunters, not wildlife lovers. It refers to how hard these animals were to hunt: they all tend to get very aggressive when you shoot at them. (And who can blame them?) They are now protected animals.

Tourists get up close with elephants

ZOOS AND GAME RESERVES

Visiting a zoo or game reserve is a good way to see a lot of South Africa's animals in a short time:

Pretoria Zoo

Pretoria Zoo is the biggest in the country and attracts over a million visitors a year. One of the highlights is an overhead cable car, from which you can look down on the animals in their large enclosures.

Kruger Game Drives

Kruger National Park is one of Africa's largest game reserves. A week's safari here is very expensive so get saving! A better alternative might be a sunset game drive into the park.

Kruger National Park wildlife

LANDSCAPE AND NATURE

SEA LIFE SOUTH AFRICA

Diving off the coast of South Africa

South Africa has an amazing variety of sea life, from the kelp forests in the cold waters off Cape Town to the tropical reefs off the coast of KwaZulu Natal. Lots of companies run diving courses and trips (real thrill seekers can even cage-dive with great white sharks). There is a simpler, cheaper way to see South Africa's sea life, though: with fins, a mask and a snorkel.

WHALE WATCHING AT HERMANUS

Between August and November, hundreds of southern right whales breed in Walkers Bay, Western Cape. The nearby town of Hermanus claims to be the best place in the world to see whales from land. Walk down to the waterfront and you'll see them out in the bay, leaping into the air, sticking their tails out of the water, or popping their heads up to have a look around.

TOP TIP – SNORKEL SAFE

Before going in the water, always check with a local diving shop or lifeguard that you're snorkelling in a safe place. Some areas are known for currents, shark attacks or other hazards – it pays to make sure you aren't in one of them!

TOP SPOTS FOR SNORKELLING

There are great snorkelling locations all along the coastline of South Africa. This is a selection of just a few:

Aliwal Shoal
(KwaZulu Natal)

The coral reefs, shipwrecks and amazing variety of sea life off the coast of KwaZulu Natal make this a paradise for underwater explorers. Aliwal Shoal is 3 km offshore, and a good place to spot dolphins, whales and even whale sharks.

Nelson Mandela Bay
(Eastern Cape)

The waters around the Cape can be chilly! The Eastern Cape is a little warmer, and at Nelson Mandela Bay you might even meet a few tropical fish. The old pier is a great place for octopus spotting.

Sodwana Bay
(KwaZulu Natal)

Once voted one of the world's top three snorkelling spots, with over 1,200 kinds of fish, beautiful coral reefs and water that's warm enough for snorkelling at any time of year.

Mossel Bay
(Southern Cape)

Mossel Bay is especially good for snorkeling because the reef is shallow. You can get up close and personal with all sorts of sea life.

Coney Glen, Knysna
(Western Cape)

Great for the less confident, as there is sunny, warm snorkelling in the area's rock pools. Watch out for the rare Knysna seahorse!

LANDSCAPE AND NATURE

Snorkelling alongside a whale shark

FOOTBALL CRAZY

South Africans go crazy for sports, and the one they go craziest for is football – though they call it soccer. It's by far the most popular sport in the country. Showing off a little knowledge of the local team is usually a good way to start a conversation with a South African.

Football is played throughout South Africa

BAFANA BAFANA

Bafana Bafana means 'the boys, the boys'. It's the nickname of the national team. If you get a chance to go and see them play, it will be a great experience. The Soccer City stadium in Johannesburg, for example, holds 94,000 people! When they start cheering, singing, shouting and drumming, the atmosphere is unforgettable.

PREMIER DIVISION

This is South Africa's top professional football league. There are 16 teams, and the season runs from August to May. Each team plays the others twice, once at their home stadium and once away. They get three points for a win, one for a draw, and none for a loss. If you can't get to see a match live, they are shown on TV on Wednesday and Friday nights, and on Saturdays and Sundays.

OTHER TEAM SPORTS

Cricket and rugby are also both very popular. The country has also produced high-level international teams and competitors in hockey, netball, athletics and swimming.

Overexcited Mamelodi Sundowns fan

SOUTH AFRICA'S TOP SOCCER TEAMS

KAIZER CHIEFS*

Home stadium: Soccer City, Johannesburg

Nickname: Amakhosi ('lords' or 'chiefs')

The biggest, most successful club in the region, with an estimated 16 million supporters spread across southern Africa.

*No, not the band – though the band WAS named after the team.

ORLANDO PIRATES*

Home stadium: Orlando Stadium, Soweto

Nickname: The Sea Robbers

The Pirates are the Kaizer Chiefs' great rivals. The club's name was inspired by the 1940 film *The Sea Hawk*, starring Errol Flynn.

*No, not Orlando, Florida, home of Walt Disney World.

MAMELODI SUNDOWNS

Home stadium: Lucas Moripe Stadium, Pretoria

Nickname: The Brazilians

Playing in the same colours as the Brazilian national team, the Sundowns had a lot to live up to. Fortunately, by 2012 they had won the Premier Division five times.

SUPERSPORT UNITED

Home stadium: Lucas Moripe Stadium, Pretoria

Nickname: Matsatsantsa ('The Swanky Boys')

The club has a strong youth academy, which has produced some top players, and has won the Premier Division several times.

ADVENTURE SPORTS

Jordy Smith, South Africa's biggest surfing star

South Africa is one of the world's adventure-sports hot spots. It has giant waves, steep mountain slopes, fast-flowing rivers and wide-open countryside – which means that whatever kind of extreme sport you're into, you can practise it here. Unless it requires snow, that is...

SURFING

South Africa is one of the world's best surfing destinations. People travel from far and wide to ride the waves. You can paddle into your first-ever wave at the gentle beach break of Muizenberg, or watch the experts try to catch monster surf at Jeffries Bay.

A small-wave day at Jeffries Bay

SHARK SAFETY

South Africa's oceans contain great whites and bull sharks – both man-eaters. These tips should help you to avoid becoming sharkbait:

- Don't go in the sea around sunrise or sunset

- Avoid surfing at river mouths or in places where the seabed drops away steeply

- Don't wee in the sea: there is evidence that this attracts sharks.

BIKING

Mountain biking and road biking are excellent in South Africa. One of the highlights of the road-biking year is the Cape Argus ride. About 35,000 riders complete the 100+ km course around the beautiful Cape Peninsula, south of Cape Town.

For off-road riders, the Cape Epic is the big attraction. The 8-day race covers about 750 km, and follows a new route each year. Riders enter in teams of two, and the event is known as one of the biggest challenges in the mountain-biking world.

Nearing the end of the Cape Epic mountain-bike race

ROCK CLIMBING

The steep slopes rising up to South Africa's central plateau are great for rock climbing. One of the best-known spots is the oddly named Restaurant At The End Of The Universe, near Johannesburg. There are over 500 routes, suitable for everyone from beginners to experts. Other good rock climbing places include the crags around Table Mountain and the Drakensberg in KwaZulu Natal.

WHITEWATER RAFTING

Several rivers in South Africa have good whitewater sections for rafters and kayakers. They include the Orange, Doring, Unkomaas and Buffalo rivers.

Whitewater kayaking on the Orange River

KEY INFORMATION
FOR TRAVELLERS

LANGUAGE

South Africa has 11 official languages: Afrikaans, English, and 9 African languages. English is widely spoken: people who do not speak it as their first language often speak it as a second.

ENTERING SOUTH AFRICA

Your passport must be valid for at least 60 days after your planned departure from South Africa, or you won't be allowed in. Visitors from the UK, USA, Canada and Australia do not need a visa, as long as they are staying fewer than 90 days.

HEALTH

The biggest danger to health is the sun, which can be very strong, causing sunburn or even sunstroke. Wear a hat, and use a minimum factor-50 sunscreen.

It's a good idea to avoid swimming in slow-moving or non-moving water, as diseases called bilharzia and cholera may be present.

If you get ill or are injured, healthcare is good in most towns and cities. In rural areas this may not be the case: you could be a long way from the nearest doctor or hospital. Do not be surprised if a doctor asks for payment in cash before he or she will treat you. Travel insurance that gives good health cover is important.

The tap water in South Africa is safe to drink, and standards of food hygiene are usually good. The local milk, dairy products, meat, fish and vegetables should all be safe to consume. Some travellers do get diarrhoea: if you have a sensitive stomach, avoid uncooked food unless it can be peeled.

POSTAL SERVICES

The national post service is the South Africa Post Office. Post offices in towns and cities are usually open Monday to Friday 08:30–15:30, and on Saturday mornings.

MOBILE NETWORKS

Use of mobile phones is growing rapidly in South Africa. The coverage is generally good, though may be tricky in isolated rural areas. Roaming on your home contract is possible but expensive: make sure you turn off data roaming.

INTERNET PROVISION

In bigger towns and cities, Internet access is generally good. Hotels and cafés may charge quite heavily for Wifi access, though: the cheapest way to get online is usually at an Internet café.

STAYING SAFE

Some areas of South Africa, particularly in cities, are quite dangerous to visit. There are a lot of guns in the country, which means a bad situation can get worse very quickly. These tips will help you to stay safe:

- Keep valuables such as cameras, phones, tablets, jewellery or expensive handbags out of sight, and do not carry large amounts of cash.

- Avoid walking at night, or along deserted streets or beaches. Stick to well-lit areas where there are other people around.

- Stay alert at traffic lights, where carjackings often happen. If a robbery does happen, keep your hands where the robbers can see them. Otherwise they may think you are reaching for a gun and shoot you.

PUBLIC HOLIDAYS

1 January	New Year's Day
21 March	Human Rights Day
Good Friday: dates change	Good Friday
Monday after Good Friday	Family Day
April: dates change	Freedom Day
1 May	Workers' Day
June: dates change	Youth Day
9 August	National Women's Day
24 September	Heritage Day
16 December	Day of Reconciliation
25 December	Christmas Day
26 December	Day of Goodwill

THE ESSENTIALS

CURRENCY:

South African rand, symbol ZAR or R (€1=R13, £1=R16, $1=R10). ATM cash withdrawal is possible in most places, including many petrol stations, where bankcards are also accepted. You can get local money at banks, airports and official moneychangers. Never withdraw money if you feel there are suspicious people hanging around.

OPENING HOURS:

There are no general opening hours for South African businesses: they vary widely. Most businesses will be open between 09:00 and 18:00 Monday to Friday as a minimum, with many open longer and at weekends.

TELEPHONE DIALLING CODES:

To call South Africa from outside the country, add the exit code from your country (from the UK this is 00), add 27 to the beginning of the number, and drop the zero from the city code.

To call another country from South Africa, add 00 and the country code of the place you are dialing to the beginning of the number, and drop the zero.

TIME ZONE:

South African Standard Time (SAST) is two hours ahead of Greenwich Mean Time. South Africa uses this throughout the year, with no daylight saving time during winter.

BOOKS TO READ: NON-FICTION

Kaffir Boy: An Autobiography Mark Mathabane (Free Press, 1986)
This book is a recognised classic. It tells the story of a young boy growing up under South Africa's brutal apartheid régime.

South Africa Alison Brownlie Bojang (Franklin Watts, 2012)
Full of interesting information about the physical features, daily life, industry, media and leisure activities of South Africa.

Long Walk To Freedom Nelson Mandela with Chris Van Wyk (Macmillan Children's Books, 2010)
Nelson Mandela's autobiography, specially shortened with the help of Chris Van Wyk to make it accessible to young readers. A great place to find out about the history of apartheid and how it was finally ended.

FINDING OUT MORE

BOOKS TO READ: FICTION

Journey To Jo'Burg Beverley Naidoo (HarperCollins, 1999)
Thirteen-year-old Naledi and her younger brother Tiro are worried that their baby sister will die. They run away from their grandmother's, where all three children live, to find their mother. But she works as a maid in Johannesburg, and getting there in apartheid South Africa is not as easy as you'd think...

No Turning Back Beverley Naidoo (Puffin, 1997)
The story of a boy who is forced to live on the street. An excellent book about apartheid South Africa.

Lost Boys Willem Van Der Walt (Oxford University Press Southern Africa, 1998)
The story of two young men, Jan and Alpha, who want to escape from the poverty of life in the Cape Flats. While Jan wants to go to university, Alpha gets involved in a criminal gang – and as if that doesn't make life complicated enough, Jan has an abandoned baby to look after.

Zulu Dog Anton Ferreira (Farrar, Strauss and Giroux, 2002)
Vusu is 11 years old when he finds a helpless bush-dog puppy all alone. He takes it in and hides it from his mother, who doesn't like dogs. The adventures of Vusu and his dog will affect the fate of his whole family. The book shows a realistic picture of what life was like after apartheid for many black South Africans.

WEBSITES

www.southafrica.com
This is the official tourist guide to South Africa. It contains excellent guides to South Africa's main cities and regions, with lots of information about things to do, the best beaches, game reserves and more. There are good sections on hiking and surfing.

www.sahikes.co.za
The site has information about over 350 different trails across South Africa. Despite being headlined 'South African Hikes', you can search the trails according to whether you're interested in hiking, 4x4, horse riding, cycling or even canoeing! It's a great site for dreaming about the outdoor adventures you might have when you visit South Africa.

tinyurl.com/yvwhje
This link will take you to the CIA (Central Intelligence Agency) web page about South Africa. It's quite dry, but crammed full of useful information and statistics.

Note to parents and teachers:
Every effort has been made by the Publishers to ensure that these websites are suitable for children, that they are of the highest educational value, and that they contain no inappropriate or offensive material. However, because of the nature of the Internet, it is impossible to guarantee that the contents of these sites will not be altered. We strongly advise that Internet access is supervised by a responsible adult.

THE ESSENTIALS

INDEX